I'm Saved!

Now What???

By

Dr. Bo Wagner

Word of His Mouth Publishers
Mooresboro, NC

All Scripture quotations are taken from the **King James Version** of the Bible.

ISBN: 987-0-9856042-4-0
Printed in the United States of America
©2012 Dr. Bo Wagner (Robert Arthur Wagner)

Word of His Mouth Publishers
PO Box 256
Mooresboro, NC 28114
704-477-5439
www.wordofhismouth.com

Table of Content

1
What Just Happened?

If you are receiving this book, then please allow me to congratulate you! Also, please allow me to give a "Whoop, Glory!" You see, the greatest thing ever has just happened, and since God could not be more happy for you, I feel the exact same way. You have just accepted Jesus Christ as your Lord and Savior. You may have heard the preacher call it "getting saved" or "being born again" or "making a profession of faith." Any of those terms are fine. They all mean the same thing in that you were on your way to Hell but now you are on your way to Heaven! Whoop, whoop, glory!

What has just happened to you may have left you walking on air, or smiling and laughing, or maybe even crying your eyes out. Different people have different emotions at a great big time like this! The emotions are not what we need to discuss for now. What we need to discuss is exactly what happened when you asked Jesus to come into your heart. We don't just want you to "feel that something special has happened," we want you to *know exactly what has happened!*

To begin with, I need to explain to you what you were before you asked Jesus into your heart. The Bible says that you were a sinner.

Romans 5:12 *Wherefore, as by one man sin entered into the world, and death by sin; and so death passed upon all men, for that all have sinned:*

Romans 3:23 *For all have sinned, and come short of the glory of God;*

These verses tell us that even if you were a nice, respectable person by the standards of our society, you were still a lost person on your way to Hell. You and God were separated from each other.

Isaiah 59:2 *But your iniquities have separated between you and your God, and your sins have hid his face from you, that he will not hear.*

Cut off from God, you were incapable of fixing things by all of the methods that men try. You could not make things better by joining a church or being baptized or being confirmed or going to confession or giving money or keeping the Ten Commandments or by making your good works outweigh your bad works. The Bible says:

Ephesians 2:8 *For by grace are ye saved through faith; and that not of yourselves: it is the gift of God:* **9 Not of works**, *lest any man should boast.*

Isaiah 64:6 *But we are all as an unclean thing, and* **all our righteousnesses are as filthy rags***; and we all do fade as a leaf; and our iniquities, like the wind, have taken us away.*

Those two verses tell us clearly that no good works that a person ever does can save him or even help to save him. All of the best things that we can do are filthy and dirty to God! So, since you had so much sinful baggage and couldn't get rid of any of it, the Lord Jesus came down to Earth and paid a terribly high price to pay for everything you ever did wrong. The Bible says:

Romans 5:8 *But God commendeth* **(that word means "demonstrated")** *his love toward us, in that, while we were yet sinners, Christ died for us.*

Simply put, everything you ever did wrong, everything you ever will do wrong, Jesus paid for it when He died on the cross. If you have ever lied, smoked, done drugs, stolen, gossiped, had a bad attitude, or even murdered someone, Jesus paid for all of it!

And then you did it. You came to an altar (or maybe it was somewhere else, the place doesn't matter a bit), and you asked the Lord to come into your heart and to forgive you of all of your sin. When you did, you were given a bath, a very special bath, in His blood:

Revelation 1:5 *And from Jesus Christ, who is the faithful witness, and the first begotten of the dead, and the prince of the kings of the earth. Unto him that loved us, and **washed us from our sins in his own blood**,*

When you asked Jesus to forgive you and come into your heart, He washed you on the inside. He used His blood to scrub away every bad thing you have ever done, every bad thought you have ever had, and everything wrong you will ever do for the rest of your life. The book of Colossians puts it this way:

Colossians 2:13 *And you, being dead in your sins and the uncircumcision of your flesh, hath he quickened* **(that word means "made alive")** *together with him, **having forgiven you all trespasses;***

When you got saved, that "blood bath" washed away all of your sins. They are gone. You don't have to feel guilty anymore *because you aren't guilty anymore!* The Bible has a great word in it that you need to know. Here is one verse where that great word is found:

Romans 5:1 *Therefore being **justified** by faith, we have peace with God through our Lord Jesus Christ:*

Let me give you a very simple definition for that word "justified." You can think of it as meaning "Just as if I had never sinned!" Now that you are saved, when God sees you He sees you as if you had never even sinned to begin with.

But having your sins done away with is not the only thing that just happened to you. You also got out of having to go to an awful place called Hell! I think you will agree that this is a very good thing. Here is how the Bible describes it:

Luke 16:23 *And in hell he lift up his eyes, being in torments, and seeth Abraham afar off, and Lazarus in his bosom.* **24** *And he cried and said, Father Abraham, have mercy on me, and send Lazarus, that he may dip the tip of his finger in water, and cool my tongue; for I am tormented in this flame.*

Hell is a very real place with very real fire. It is the agonizing and eternal home of anyone that refuses to accept Christ as his or her Savior. But the good news is, you no longer have to worry about that! The Bible says:

John 5:24 *Verily, verily* **(that word means "truly")**, *I say unto you, He that heareth my word, and believeth on him that sent me,*

9

hath everlasting life, and shall not come into condemnation; but is passed from death unto life.

You will never have to be condemned to Hell; you have passed from death (being lost) unto life (being saved)!

Another thing that just happened to you is that you just received a place to live in Heaven! I don't know what kind of a house you live in here, but I do know what kind of a house you will live in for all of eternity.

John 14:1 *Let not your heart be troubled: ye believe in God, believe also in me.* **2** *In my Father's house are many mansions: if it were not so, I would have told you. I go to prepare a place for you.* **3** *And if I go and prepare a place for you, I will come again, and receive you unto myself; that where I am, there ye may be also.*

You get to go to Heaven; you get to live in a mansion forever!

But there is yet another thing that you should know about what happened. Look at this verse:

2 Corinthians 5:17 *Therefore if any man be in Christ, he is a new creature: old things are passed away; behold, all things are become new.*

When you got saved, the "old you" died! You became a brand new person when you asked Jesus to save you. What does that mean?

Well, one thing that it *doesn't mean* is that you will no longer have to deal with the earthly consequences of your past actions. If you robbed a bank before you came to the altar today, I'm sorry to inform you that you are in fact going to go to jail, regardless of the fact that you got saved! What it does mean, though, is that you no longer have to fear any judgment from God for your past actions. Jesus was punished for what you did, and God is not going to punish the same sin more than once!

Another thing it means is that you now have someone living inside of you. Whoa! That is a scary thought! But hold on, let me explain it, and it won't be near as scary. The Bible says:

1 Corinthians 6:19 *What? know ye not that your body is the temple of the Holy Ghost which is in you, which ye have of God, and ye are not your own?*

Romans 8:9 *But ye are not in the flesh, but in the Spirit, if so be that the Spirit of God dwell in you. Now if any man have not the Spirit of Christ, he is none of his.*

Before you asked Jesus to save you, you were on your own when it came to trying to live right. No wonder you couldn't do it! But when you got saved, the Holy Spirit came to live inside of you. As a sinner you could sin, and it probably did not bother you much. But you will now find that as a Christian, that is no longer true. When you sin now (and you will) you will find yourself very uncomfortable, even miserable! It will be like there is a voice inside your head saying, "No! No! No! You can't do that!" You see, the Holy Spirit has a job when it comes to Christians. His job is to make them miserable when they do wrong so that they will do right instead. You never had that before, but you do now!

Another thing it means is that you will find yourself drawn to things that you may never have had much use for before. The things that God loves (things like the Bible, church, prayer, hanging around Christians) you will begin to love those things too. And the things that God doesn't like (things like drinking, cursing, sleeping around, doing drugs) will suddenly feel sort of dirty to you.

Does this mean that you will never sin again? No. You are saved on the inside, but you are still trapped in a body that has spent a lot of time learning to like doing wrong! That is going to make for a conflict that we will talk about later. But for now, let's just smile and celebrate for a bit. You just got saved, which means that:

Everything bad you have ever done has been paid for.

You have been washed clean in Jesus' blood.

You aren't guilty anymore.

You don't have to go to Hell.

You get to go to Heaven.

The old you is gone.

The Holy Spirit is now living in your heart.

You will find yourself drawn to things you may never have had much use for before.

Is there more? You bet! But that's enough for this chapter. Congratulations on getting saved, and welcome to the family!

2
What Do I Need to Do First?

That is an excellent question; I'm so glad you asked! Getting saved did a lot of things *for* you. But now there are some things that you will need to do *because* you got saved. The very first thing is called "getting baptized." Let me explain what that means, what it doesn't mean, and why you need to do it.

Let me first of all re-assure you that if you accepted Christ, you are saved, and nothing else needs to be done about that. Getting baptized does not get a person saved. Getting baptized does not get a person "more saved." Not getting baptized does not make a person lose his or her salvation. Look with me at the account of a man who got saved under Jesus' ministry:

Luke 23:39 *And one of the malefactors* **(that word means "evil doers")** *which hanged railed on him, saying, If thou be Christ,* *save thyself and us.* **40** *But the other answering rebuked him, saying, Dost not thou fear God, seeing thou art in the same condemnation?* **41** *And we indeed justly; for we receive the due reward of our deeds: but this man hath done nothing amiss.* **42** *And he said unto Jesus, Lord, remember me when thou comest into thy kingdom.* **43** *And Jesus said unto him, Verily I say unto thee, To day shalt thou be with me in paradise.*

This happened while Jesus was dying on Calvary. A man hanging on another cross beside him accepted Christ into his heart, and without ever having a chance to get baptized, he got saved and got to go to Heaven. Always remember then, that as important as baptism is, it has absolutely nothing to do with getting a person saved!

Baptism is simply the very first step of obedience for a new Christian. Everyone who got saved in the Bible understood this.

Acts 8:36 *And as they went on their way, they came unto a certain water: and the eunuch said, See, here is water; what doth hinder me to be baptized?* **37** *And Philip said, If thou believest with all thine heart, thou mayest. And he answered and said, I believe that Jesus Christ is the Son of God.* **38** *And he commanded the chariot to stand still: and they went down* *both into the water, both Philip and the eunuch; and he baptized him.*

Immediately after believing on Jesus, this man was baptized. God commanded His people to include baptism in what they did.

Matthew 28:19 *Go ye therefore, and teach all nations, baptizing them in the name of the Father, and of the Son, and of the Holy Ghost:*

This is not an optional thing. You can be saved without being baptized, but you cannot be "right with God" without being baptized. When we talk about being right with God, we mean being obedient to Him so that He can bless your life. You have gotten saved, now you need to obey Him and be baptized, and you need to do so as soon as possible.

So what is this thing called baptism? Well, the word baptize literally means "to dunk under the water." You may have seen or heard of people sprinkling people with water or pouring water on them and calling it baptism. I'm not trying to hurt any feelings but that isn't actually baptism. Look at how the Bible always describes baptism:

Matthew 3:16 *And Jesus, when he was baptized, went up straightway **out of the water**: and, lo, the heavens were opened unto him, and he saw the Spirit of God descending like a dove, and lighting upon him:*

Mark 1:10 *And straightway coming up* ***out of the water****, he saw the heavens opened, and the Spirit like a dove descending upon him:*

Acts 8:39 *And when they were come up* ***out of the water****, the Spirit of the Lord caught away Philip, that the eunuch saw him no more: and he went on his way rejoicing.*

You can also see this in John's baptism ministry in a place called Aenon.

John 3:23 *And John also was baptizing in Aenon near to Salim, because there was* ***much water*** *there: and they came, and were baptized.*

There is no need for *much water* in baptism unless you are dunking people under water!

The main reason that God chose "dunking under the water" as baptism is because of what it symbolizes.

Romans 6:3 *Know ye not, that so many of us as were baptized into Jesus Christ were baptized into his death?* **4** *Therefore we are* ***buried*** *with him by baptism into death: that like as Christ was raised up from the dead by the glory of the Father, even so we also should walk in newness of life.* **5** *For if we have been planted together in the likeness of his death, we shall be also in the likeness of his resurrection:*

Colossians 2:12 ***Buried*** *with him in baptism, wherein also ye are risen with him* *through the faith of the operation of God, who hath raised him from the dead.*

Notice that word "buried" in both verses. Do you remember how I told you that when you got saved the old you died, and you became someone brand new? Well, what do you do with someone that has died? You *bury them.* And then, if that person came back to life, what would you do? *Bring them back up!* Baptism symbolizes this. When you go under the water, it is a picture of the old you, the sinner, dying at the altar where you accepted Christ. When you are brought back up out of the water, it is a picture of the new you that came to life in place of the old you that died! This is a very powerful symbol and a very strong way to let everyone know what has happened to you.

So what you should do now is talk to the pastor and set up a time to get baptized. When you do, invite everyone you know out to see you get baptized. Who knows, you may end up seeing many of your family and friends get saved during that service just because they came out to see you get baptized!

3
You Need to Get in Church, Fast!

Please, let me give you your first piece of bad news since the moment that you got saved. The bad news is, you just made an enemy, a very powerful enemy.

1 Peter 5:8 *Be sober, be vigilant; because your adversary the devil, as a roaring lion, walketh about, seeking whom he may devour:*

The devil himself now wants to tear you apart! Oh well, good luck with that, I'm out of here! No, I'm just kidding. I'm not about to leave you alone with a problem like that. I'm going to tell you exactly what you need to do about this new enemy of yours.

First of all, let me reassure you that the devil cannot take you to Hell. You are on your way to Heaven, and he has no power to stop that. What he can do, if you let him, is to wreck your life in the mean time. He probably did not mess with you much before, because you already belonged to him! But now that you belong to the Lord, he will definitely try and cause problems in your life. And that is one of the main reasons that you need to get in church, fast!

Let me tell you a story, and you see what you think of it:

A man and woman once had a baby, a precious, wide-eyed, wrinkled-up little bundle of joy. Like all newborns, he was helpless. He could not walk, talk, feed himself, keep himself clean, and he certainly couldn't defend himself. And so, his mom and dad did the only reasonable thing: they took him outside and left him laying on the sidewalk to fend for himself. The end.

I know what you are thinking: "That is the worst story ever! How could a mom and dad leave a helpless little baby alone like that, exposed to danger, where it could be eaten by animals or stolen by a creep?" Excellent question. And the answer is, no good parent would ever do that! Every good parent takes very good care of newborn babies. And here is where I am going with that line of thinking:

1 Peter 2:2 *As newborn babes, desire the sincere milk of the word, that ye may grow thereby:*

When you got saved you became a newborn baby! You are what the Bible calls a "babe in Christ." You have no spiritual strength yet, no ability to defend yourself against the attacks of the devil; you need some help! And that is where a local church comes in. One of the jobs of the church is to teach you, train you, and help you to grow up into a mature Christian, capable of defending yourself against the attacks of the devil.

Just like baptism, you cannot be right with God without it! You will (probably very soon) meet people who claim to be right with the Lord, yet who do not go to church. Despite what they say, they are absolutely not right with the Lord if they do not go to church! Here is what the Bible says:

Hebrews 10:25 *Not forsaking the assembling of ourselves together, as the manner of some is; but exhorting one another: and so much the more, as ye see the day approaching.*

Nehemiah 10:39b *...and we will not forsake the house of our God.*

Psalm 122:1 *I was glad when they said unto me, Let us go into the house of the LORD.*

All of these verses are talking about our attendance in God's house, which is now called the church. God feels very strongly about the local church.

Matthew 16:18b *...upon this rock I will build my church; and the gates of hell shall not prevail against it.*

Acts 20:28 *Take heed therefore unto yourselves, and to all the flock, over the which the Holy Ghost hath made you overseers, to feed the church of God, which he hath purchased with his own blood.*

Ephesians 5:25 *Husbands, love your wives, even as Christ also loved the church, and gave himself for it;*

Jesus loves the church, and if you don't love the things that He loves, then you don't love Him! You need to be in church every time they are having service. Most churches will have Sunday school, Sunday morning service that immediately follows Sunday school, a Sunday night service, and a Wednesday night service. That may sound like a lot, but it is only about 4 hours out of a 168-hour week! Another way to put it is, that is only about 2% of your week. Not much!

Each of these services will do something for you, and each of them are designed a bit differently. Sunday school is a teaching time, when you will learn the facts and figure about your Bible. Some of the other services will be used as a time to try to win more people to the Lord, some of them will be used to encourage those that are down and out, and some will be used to tell people what things are sin and to stay away from those things. All of the services of a local church, every single one of them, are really important! If you want to grow and learn and eventually be able to help others, you need to be in every single service, even special services like revival meetings.

But you need to do more than just attend church. You need to actually become a part of it. You need to ask the pastor how you can become a member of the church. Some churches handle that a bit differently than others. Some will tell you that you become a member when you get baptized. Others will tell you that you need to come and stand before the church to be voted in. Whichever way they handle it, do it! Just attending a church is not quite good enough; you need to be an active part of it. Here is what the Bible says:

1 Corinthians 12:12 *For as the body is one, and hath many members, and all the members of that one body, being many, are one body: so also is Christ.*

In other words, you don't just need to be a long-term visitor to the body (the church), you need to be a member of it! A tick is a long-term visitor to the body, and who would ever appreciate that, other than the tick? You need to become a part of the body so that you can be a help to the body, and the body can be a help to you.

Church members encourage each other when they are down. Church members pray for each other. Church members laugh and cry with each other. Church members become the best of friends. Church members will lovingly confront you when you start to do something wrong or when you get slack in your relationship with the Lord. When it comes to people, you will never find a perfect church, but you will also never find anything more perfect than the church!

Join a good church, fast!

4
What Do I Do with this Bible Thing?

People these days are really not very familiar with the Bible anymore. In years gone by, even lost people knew a great deal about it. But these days, even those that claim to be saved do not seem to know much about it at all. You may have noticed that it is pretty important to us. We are always preaching from it, quoting it, and checking to see what it says on different things. You will notice that I have printed a whole lot of verses from it in just the first few pages of this book! Now that you are saved, you really need to know what you have when it comes to the Bible and what you should do with it.

To begin with, let me tell you what the Bible is. This is very important; it is foundational. **The Bible is the Word of God, and it is the only Word of God**. With so many

27

religions having so many other books, you really need to get settled on this one fact very quickly!

The Bible itself is not a bit "wishy-washy" on this issue. If you ask your Bible what it is, here is what it will tell you:

Genesis 15:1 *After these things **the word of the LORD** came unto Abram...*

Are you ready for this? The Bible calls itself the "Word of the LORD" 258 times! Here is something else the Bible calls itself:

Luke 4:4 *And Jesus answered him, saying, It is written, That man shall not live by bread alone, but by every **word of God**.*

The Bible calls itself the "Word of God" 49 times! And here is how we got it:

2 Peter 1:21 *For the prophecy came not in old time by the will of man: but holy men of God spake as they were moved by the Holy Ghost.*

God literally told the human writers of the 66 books of the Bible exactly what to write. That is why every word in the Bible is perfect! Men make mistakes when they write books, but God makes no mistakes. But what about other religious books? How do we know that the Bible is the Word of God and that those other books are wrong?

Well, the Bible has the proof, while the others don't! Here are some reasons how we know that the Bible is God's Word.

First, let's consider the way it was written. The Bible is clearly one long story, from creation till the end of time and on into eternity. When you read it from front to back, it makes perfect sense. But consider this: it took 1600 years to write. It was written by over 40 different authors. Among them were a political leader, some fishermen, a military general, a cupbearer, a prime minister, a doctor, several kings, a tax collector, and an ex-rabbi. It was written in a wilderness, a dungeon, a palace, a prison, a ship, and on an island. It was written on three different continents and in three different languages. Yet for all of this, there are no contradictions, no errors, and only one theme throughout, Jesus, Jesus, Jesus! If any other book had been written the way the Bible was written, it would be a jumbled mess! All of the other religious books on Earth were written very quickly, usually by just one person, and they still all have errors all the way through them! We know the Bible is God's Word because of the miraculous way it was written.

We also know the Bible is God's Word because of how indestructible it has proven to be.   A wicked Roman emperor named Diocletian in A. D. 303 attempted to destroy all of the Bibles in the empire. He built a column which said, "Extinct is the name Christian." Today, everyone knows the word Christian and most everyone has access to a Bible, but few have ever heard of Diocletian. Hitler tried to burn and ban it. An atheist named Voltaire said, "Another century and there will not be one Bible on Earth." Years later, his house was being used as a place to print Bibles! Joseph Stalin instituted a "Ban the Bible Purge" in the USSR. Yet today, while Stalin's body rots in the grave and his soul burns in Hell, Bibles are flooding that country by the millions.

We also know that the Bible is God's Word because of its fulfilled prophecies. This one thing alone makes the Bible the most unique book on Earth! The Bible did not make general, vague prophecies that someone could later twist into saying, "See! There it is!" The Bible made very specific and very *unlikely* prophecies, all of which either have come to pass or are in the process of coming to pass. Here are just a few of them that have already been specifically fulfilled:

The defeat of Persia, predicted 225 years ahead of time - Daniel 8:7.

The early death of Alexander the Great, predicted 230 years ahead of time - Daniel 8:8.

The birthplace of Jesus, predicted 710 years ahead of time - Micah 5:2.

The virgin birth, predicted 700 years ahead of time - Isaiah 7:14.

The detailed sufferings of Christ on the cross, predicted 1000 years ahead of time - Psalm 22.

Would you like for me to give you a list of all of the specific, detailed prophecies that the other religious books on Earth have predicted and then had fulfilled? Here they are:

That's it! Zip, zilch, nada, zero, none! No other religious book on Earth has any detailed fulfilled prophecies to point to, only the Bible! Why? Because the Bible is the only book that God wrote.

Archaeology and science also tell us clearly which book is the Word of God. In the mid 1800s, the Encyclopedia Britannica said that the Hittite nation never existed, yet the Bible mentions them many, many times. Less than 70 years later, archaeologists found the ruins, which are now among the most extensive of any ancient civilization. When the city of Jericho was found, the walls had fallen flat, just as Joshua 6:20 said. Christopher Columbus was motivated to sail the seas when he realized that God's Word proclaimed the world as round and not flat.

Isaiah 40:22 *It is he that sitteth upon **the circle of the earth**, and the inhabitants thereof are as grasshoppers; that stretcheth out the heavens as a curtain, and spreadeth them out as a tent to dwell in:*

Isaiah wrote these words 2,200 years before Columbus sailed the ocean blue!

Ancient man believed that the world rested on the back of a large turtle or on the shoulders of a giant, yet the Bible taught that the Earth hung upon nothing.

Job 26:7 *He stretcheth out the north over the empty place, and hangeth the earth upon nothing.*

This was not written in the 21st century; Job was the oldest Bible book ever put into writing! And Job was not done yet. Thousands of years before submarines, God told of fresh water springs in the sea.

Job 38:16 *Hast thou entered into the springs of the sea? or hast thou walked in the search of the depth?*

These springs were not found until the 20th century, yet God wrote about them 3,500 years ago!

The Bible is the Word of God, and it is the *only Word of God.* Look at what God said:

Galatians 1:8 *But though we, or an angel from heaven, preach any other gospel unto you than that which we have preached unto you, let him be accursed.* **9** *As we said before, so say I now again, If any man preach any other gospel unto you than that ye have received, let him be accursed.*

God said that even if an angel shows up and tells you that he has another message from God for you, don't believe him. Let him be "accursed!" That is interesting since two of the biggest cults in the world, Islam and the Mormons, both claim to have been given their religious books from angels!

What you have, new Christian, is the Word of God. But that brings us to our next question. What should you do with it? Well, the obvious first answer is, READ IT! But let me give you a few pointers, please. With most books you will want to start at the beginning and read all the way to the end. You will eventually want to do that with your Bible, but not just yet. There are many things in the Bible that are very confusing to a new Christian. I think the best thing that you can do is to start at the simplest spot and begin there.

The Bible is divided into what is called the Old Testament and the New Testament. Go to the New Testament and start in the book of Matthew. The first four books of the New Testament are called the Gospels. They are all about the life and death and the resurrection of Jesus. You will read many of the same things in those first four books, since it was four different writers writing about the same set of events. Each of them, though, will cover some things that the others did not. When you are done reading those first four books, you will know a great deal about Jesus, the One Who just saved you!

After you are finished reading Matthew, Mark, Luke, and John, skip ahead to the book of Romans. Romans is a book all about Salvation. Reading that book will really help you understand what just happened to you and how you are supposed to live now. After that I recommend that you read the books of Psalms and Proverbs. From there, ask your pastor where he recommends that you read. He will probably have a good idea of what you need to read by that point from having observed you at church and in your daily life.

Not only should you read your Bible, you should start memorizing verses. The Bible says:

Psalm 119:11 *Thy word have I hid in mine heart, that I might not sin against thee.*

The more Scripture you memorize, the less likely you are to slip up and sin! A good thing to do is when you have an area you struggle with (temper, cursing, laziness, lust, etc.) ask your pastor for good verses to memorize. He will know just what verses will help you with that issue.

While you are reading your Bible, you are eventually going to come across something that makes you scratch your head and say, "Wait a minute, why don't we actually do this anymore?" Here is an example:

Leviticus 3:7 *If he offer a lamb for his offering, then shall he offer it before the LORD. 8 And he shall lay his hand upon the head of his offering, and kill it before the tabernacle of the* *congregation: and Aaron's sons shall sprinkle the blood thereof round about upon the altar.*

I am pretty sure that no matter who you are or where you are from, you have never seen anyone kill a lamb and sprinkle its blood on an altar! There are a lot of things like that in the Bible. So why don't we do that? Look at this verse:

2 Timothy 2:15 *Study to shew thyself approved unto God, a workman that needeth not to be ashamed,* **rightly dividing the word of truth**.

We are to study our Bibles and learn how to "rightly divide" it. In other words, certain things in the Bible, especially in the Old Testament, were temporary things, written to specific people. In the case of killing lambs and sprinkling blood, that was written to the Jewish people and was only to last until Jesus shed His blood on Calvary. So be very careful with your Bible. Study it, and if something makes you scratch your head, go ask your pastor to explain it to you!

5
Start to Pray, Right Away!

Ok, so you have already prayed at least one prayer; you have already prayed and asked the Lord to save you! That's good. I am guessing that you may have prayed other little prayers along the way, such as "saying grace" over a meal now and then, and maybe even an "emergency prayer" when you thought you were about to wreck your car!

But you are probably figuring out that there is a lot more to prayer than what you knew. These folks in church, they will stand up and pray out loud, they will gather at the altar and pray, they even talk about having God answer their prayers! Don't be nervous. Prayer is one of the first things you need to start doing, and it is also one of the most important, but it is not nearly as complicated as you may think.

Perhaps you have heard some people pray, and it sounds very...well, holy and worshipful. Something along the lines of a man with a British accent saying, "Oh, our great and worshipful God, we thank thee this day for thy bounty upon us..."

There is nothing at all wrong with that. But it is also not necessary for you to try to pray like that in order to actually be praying! Prayer is simply talking to God, either out loud or silently in your mind and heart. Yes, you do want to be very respectful, because it is God that you are talking to after all. But the Bible also says:

Hebrews 4:16 *Let us therefore come boldly unto the throne of grace, that we may obtain mercy, and find grace to help in time of need.*

Because you are saved, you can pray boldly! This means that you can talk to God as if you were talking to your best friend or your father, because actually, He now is both your Best Friend and your Father! Whatever you are feeling, be honest with Him and tell Him, because He already knows anyway! For instance, there is no need pretending to be happy when you pray if you are actually sad. Whatever you are scared about, tell Him. If there is something you need, ask Him.

But don't forget to do a few other things when you pray, too. For one, be sure to always spend some time thanking Him when you pray.

He has been very good to you, and it is proper for you to say thank you each and every time you pray. Thank Him for saving you, for giving you life and health, for your family, and for your job; whatever good things you have, thank Him for them. You see, the Bible says:

James 1:17 *Every good gift and every perfect gift is from above, and cometh down from the Father of lights, with whom is no variableness, neither shadow of turning.*

Every good thing we have comes from God, so when you pray, pick out a few of those good things and say thank you!

Another thing you always want to be sure to do when you pray is to apologize for any recent sins. You see, even after getting saved, you are still going to sin from time to time. That doesn't mean that you need to get saved again (I'll say more about that a few chapters from now) but it does mean that you ought to apologize. Jesus told His disciples to ask for forgiveness when they prayed.

Luke 11:2 *And he said unto them, When ye pray, say, Our Father which art in heaven, Hallowed be thy name. Thy kingdom come. Thy will be done, as in heaven, so in earth.* **3** *Give us day by day our daily bread.* **4 And forgive us our sins***; for we also forgive every one that is indebted to us. And lead us not into temptation; but deliver us from evil.*

It is never a good idea to let there be something between you and God, so when you pray, if you have done anything wrong recently, ask Him to forgive you.

One thing I want you to know about praying is that you can do it anywhere, anytime. You definitely shouldn't just wait until you get to church to pray! You also shouldn't wait until you can find a place to kneel down, bow your head, and close your eyes. The Bible says:

1 Thessalonians 5:17 *Pray without ceasing.*

This means that you should be praying all the time! You can pray while you are driving down the road (eyes open, please!); you can pray while you are laying awake in bed; you can pray while you are working; you can pray while you are fishing. There is nowhere that you cannot pray! Spend lots and lots and lots of time praying!

Now, do make sure that in addition to just praying throughout your day while you are doing other stuff, you also set aside a definite time and place to do nothing but pray. Jesus said it this way:

Matthew 6:6 *But thou, when thou prayest, enter into thy closet, and when thou hast shut thy door, pray to thy Father which is in secret; and thy Father which seeth in secret shall reward thee openly.*

It does not have to be a literal closet. You may not even be able to fit into your closet along with all of the shoes and clothes and boxes! This verse is teaching us that we need to have a quiet place and a specific time to kneel before God and pray for a while. This is your personal alone time with God, and you are going to need it. How do I know that? Because even Jesus needed it! Look at this:

Mark 1:35 *And in the morning, rising up a great while before day, he went out, and departed into a solitary place, and there prayed.*

Jesus, the Son of God and God the Son, got alone with the Father to pray. If He needed it, believe me, you do too! Your power for living will come mostly through prayer. As a Christian, there is not much more important you can ever do than pray!

6
What Are They Doing During Those Church Services?

There is a lot that goes on during a church service, and there may be much of it that you don't understand yet. That is ok, because I am going to explain some of it. Let's take it piece by piece.

Singing

You are going to find out that Christians are a "singing kind of people!" When you are in church you will probably see and hear a choir, some smaller groups, soloists, and then there will be congregational singing where everyone participates. Singing is very important in church, because it was very important in the Bible. In fact, if you turn to the very middle of your Bible, you will find the book of Psalms. It is the longest book in the Bible, and all of it is a song book! Those chapters in it are individual songs that believers in God sang during their worship services thousands of years ago. You will also find that Jesus and His disciples sang:

Matthew 26:30 *And when they had sung an hymn, they went out into the mount of Olives.*

There will also be singing in Heaven.

Revelation 14:3 *And they sung as it were a new song before the throne, and before the four beasts, and the elders: and no man could learn that song but the hundred and forty and four thousand, which were redeemed from the earth.*

Singing is very precious to God; He loves it when we sing. You may be thinking, "But I can't carry a tune in a bucket!" That's ok. The Bible says:

Psalm 66:1 *Make a joyful noise unto God, all ye lands:*

It really isn't how well you sing that matters to God. He wants you to sing out of a joyful heart. And since you are saved, you have every reason to be joyful! So when it comes time for the congregational singing, pick up the hymn book, turn to the page the song leader calls out, and jump in. You may have to listen a few times to get the tune in your head, but you will get it. And after a while, those songs will become favorites to you! You will find yourself humming and singing them at work; they will brighten your day. They will remind you of Jesus and Heaven and the day you got saved.

If you have even a reasonably decent voice, pray about joining the choir. A big strong choir is a tremendous blessing to a church, so ask your pastor about it!

Praising

This may have already made your heart skip a beat once or twice if you are not yet used to it. It is possible that you were sitting in church, minding your own business, and all of a sudden someone behind you shouted really loud! It may have been "Amen!" or "Glory to God!" or even something that sounded like a war yell! Why on Earth do people do that, and is it ok? Yes, it is ok, it is even better than ok! The Bible mentions vocal praising of God more than 800 times! Here are a few of those times:

Psalm 5:11 *But let all those that put their trust in thee rejoice: let them ever **shout for joy**, because thou defendest them: let them also that love thy name be joyful in thee.*

Luke 19:37 *And when he was come nigh, even now at the descent of the mount of Olives, the whole multitude of the disciples began to rejoice and **praise God with a loud voice** for all the mighty works that they had seen;*

Matthew 21:16 *And said unto him, Hearest thou what these say? And Jesus saith unto them, Yea; have ye never read,* **Out of the mouth of babes and sucklings thou hast perfected praise?** *17 And he left them, and went out of the city into Bethany; and he lodged there.*

The Lord loves to hear us praise Him!

Many of the words people use to praise Him have specific meanings that you should know. One of the main ones you are likely to hear is the word **Amen**. It is often used as an ending to a prayer, but it is just as often used as a word of praise. It means "so be it" or "I agree." That is why when a preacher says something good or a song has really good words, you will often hear people saying, "Amen!" They are agreeing with what has been said or sung.

Another word often used is **Hallelujah!** It basically means "Praise the Lord!" Others you might hear are **Glory to God!** or **Glory!** There are many words and even sounds that you will hear used to praise the Lord. It is good to praise the Lord. In fact, the Psalmist said the same thing four different times in one chapter alone:

Psalm 107:8 *Oh that men would praise the LORD for his goodness, and for his wonderful works to the children of men!*

Psalm 107:15 *Oh that men would praise the LORD for his goodness, and for his wonderful works to the children of men!*

Psalm 107:21 *Oh that men would praise the LORD for his goodness, and for his wonderful works to the children of men!*

Psalm 107:31 *Oh that men would praise the LORD for his goodness, and for his wonderful works to the children of men!*

If he said it four times, it must be important! It is also something that helps a service. When people praise the Lord, it does much the same thing that cheering for a team at a ball game does. It makes the atmosphere electric; it makes everything exciting! If we can't get excited about God, what in the world can we get excited about? So try it. Next service, shout out a good "Amen" or two. You will enjoy it, God will enjoy it, and it will help increase the excitement in the service.

People putting money in the offering plates

This is something you very likely have noticed by now. Sometime during the service, some men called Ushers will carry offering plates around the auditorium, and people will put money in them. They may drop in cash or a check. Some will drop in small envelopes, called offering envelopes, with their cash or checks in those. Giving during the offering time

47

is a very important part of worshiping the Lord. In fact, I bet you remember what the wise men did when they came to see the baby Jesus.

Matthew 2:11 *And when they were come into the house, they saw the young child with Mary his mother, and fell down, and worshipped him: and when they had opened their treasures, they presented unto him gifts; gold, and frankincense, and myrrh.*

Notice that the verse says they worshiped Him and that when they did so it was by giving gold, frankincense, and myrrh–three very costly things. Since God gave us so much, we who are saved do not mind giving back to Him! And that is what people are doing when they put money in the offering plate. That money is used for something that is very precious to God:

Malachi 3:10 *Bring ye all the tithes into the storehouse,* ***that there may be meat in mine house****, and prove me now herewith, saith the LORD of hosts, if I will not open you the windows of heaven, and pour you out a blessing, that there shall not be room enough to receive it.*

What goes into that offering plate is used primarily for the upkeep of the house of God. It keeps the lights on and the building payments made and the water running and whatever else is needed. But above all, it keeps people getting saved, like you just were! In order for you to get saved, people put money into the offering plate. That money allowed the lights to be on and the heat or air to be running the day that you came. It allowed for there to be a preacher studying and praying all week before he preached to you. It allowed there to be a parking lot for you to park your car on. It allowed for there to be a roof over your head so you did not get rained on while the preacher was preaching to you. There is nothing more important that a church does than to get people saved, and that cannot happen without people being willing to give!

What the people are giving is what the Bible calls a "tithe." That word means a tenth. When you see Christians giving, they will have figured out what a tenth of their income is, and that is what they will be putting in the offering plate. If their gross salary was $1000 for the week, they will be putting $100 in the offering plate.

At this point you may be thinking "Whoa! There is no way I could make ends meet like that!" Well, pay attention to what that last verse you read said. It promised that God would bless those that obey in this. Does that mean that God will make you rich? No. But it does mean that He will meet your needs.

Maybe not all of your *wants*, but He is in the habit of meeting needs.

Philippians 4:19 *But my God shall supply all your need according to his riches in glory by Christ Jesus.*

There are other ways and amounts that Christians give, like offerings for missions and such as that, but those are a bit more advanced, and your pastor will, no doubt, be explaining all of that later.

The Lord's Supper

Some times you will hear this referred to as "communion." Either way, it is the same thing. This is when there is a special service, or a special time during a service, where people eat tiny pieces of bread and drink little cups of grape juice. It is definitely not enough to fill you up, so what is it for?

Here is how the Bible describes it:

1 Corinthians 11:23 *For I have received of the Lord that which also I delivered unto you, That the Lord Jesus the same night in which he was betrayed took bread:* **24** *And when he had given thanks, he brake it, and said, Take, eat: this is my body, which is broken for you: this do in remembrance of me.* **25** *After the same manner also he took the cup, when he had supped, saying, This cup is the new testament in my blood: this do ye, as oft as ye drink it, in* *remembrance of me. 26 For as often as ye eat this bread, and drink this cup, ye do shew the Lord's death till he come. 27 Wherefore whosoever shall eat this bread, and drink this cup of the Lord, unworthily, shall be guilty of the body and blood of the Lord. 28 But let a man examine himself, and so let him eat of that bread, and drink of that cup. 29 For he that eateth and drinketh unworthily, eateth and drinketh damnation to himself, not discerning the Lord's body. 30 For this cause many are weak and sickly among you, and many sleep.*

Let me begin by telling you what the Lord's Supper is not. First of all, it is not some mystical thing where the bread and juice actually become the physical blood and flesh of Jesus. It is simply a symbol to remind us of the broken body and the shed blood of Jesus. Second, it is not a way that you get saved or "more saved" nor is it a way to "receive more grace."

So what is it? As I said, it is simply a symbol to remind us of the broken body and the shed blood of Jesus. It is a solemn service in which we think back to Calvary and memorialize what Jesus did for us there. It is also a time to check up on whether or not we are living right. According to verses 28-30, before we eat that bread or drink that juice we are to examine ourselves. We need to make sure we are not willingly sinning and not repenting of it. Anyone doing that and then taking the Lord's Supper is likely to be in for some trouble! Verse 30 tells us that we may get sick or even worse. Not taking the Lord's Supper is not really an option since God has commanded us to do it. It is what He called an "ordinance" of the local church. So, since we need to take it, the only option left to us is to apologize and forsake any sins we have been doing and then joyfully take the Lord's Supper, thanking Him for what He did for us on Calvary.

Calling each other "odd names"

When you have been in church so far, you have probably heard people refer to each other in unusual ways. A woman named Bertha may be referred to as "Sister Bertha." A man named Fred may be called "Brother Fred." You may get the idea that everybody in the church is related! And the reason for that is...they are! You see, when you got saved, God became your Father. So, since He is my Father too, that makes us spiritual siblings!

And then there is the Pastor. He will almost always be referred to without even using his name. Most people will simply call him "Pastor" or "Preacher." They may also add his last name, like "Pastor Friplethorpe" or "Preacher Jones." The reason for that is simple.

The office of the pastor is one that deserves the highest respect. That man has been called by God to do what he is doing. Because of that, young and old should always refer to him by his title.

Using unfamiliar terms

You may, by now, have heard people speaking something that sounds like a foreign language to you. They may have said, "Don't be worldly" or "Crucify the flesh!" or "Let's get hold of the horns of the altar." I could give you many more examples. The reason they talk like that is because they are using terms and phrases from the Bible, many of which people don't use on a regular basis anymore. That's ok. You yourself will learn what all of those "odd terms" mean over time.

There are a lot of other things that happen in church that you may not yet understand. When that happens, go ask your pastor to explain. He will not mind a bit!

7

How Are You Supposed to Act When You Are Not in Church?

From the preaching you have heard so far, you have probably noticed that a lot of what the pastor says deals with "Monday through Saturday living" rather than "Sunday living." That is what the Bible is really for! The Bible is not a Sunday Book; it is an every day Book. When you got saved, God expected you to start living a different kind of life, even when you are away from church. The Bible puts it this way:

1 Peter 1:15 *But as he which hath called you is holy, so be ye holy in all manner of conversation; 16 Because it is written, Be ye holy; for I am holy.*

That word "conversation" means more than just what you say with your lips. It literally means also what you say with your life! Now that you are saved, God expects you to be living a holy life. So we will need to go find you guys a monastery to live in and you girls some black "Nun clothes" to wear...

No, I'm just kidding! There is no need for those kinds of things at all; those things have nothing to do with holiness. To be holy means to stay away from sin! You are going to find a lot of things in the Bible that God said "no" to. And whatever He said "no" to, we are to stay away from! You will find that because of what the Bible says, real Christians do not drink alcohol, or do drugs, or cuss, or look at pornography, or steal, or cheat, or run around on their spouses, or a bunch of other wicked things. The list is obviously way too long for me to give you here. But long story short, now that you are saved, you need to live like it! There are a few reasons for that.

First of all, as we saw in those verses above, it is what God expects of us. And as a Christian, whatever He expects is what you need to do!

Secondly, we have something called a "testimony" to consider. The Bible says this:

Matthew 5:16 *Let your light so shine before men, that they may see your good works, and glorify your Father which is in heaven.*

In other words, people need to be able to see how clean you live, because seeing that will draw them to God. People that can't stand church and won't go to church ought to be able to hear that you got saved and then see it in the way that you live. You will become a "walking church service" to them! People will probably get saved because they see the change in you.

A third reason you ought to live clean at all times is because of what the Bible calls the Judgment Seat of Christ. Here is what the Bible says:

2 Corinthians 5:10 *For we must all appear before the judgment seat of Christ; that every one may receive the things done in his body, according to that he hath done, whether it be good or bad.*

This is a judgment that only saved people will go to. It is like the awards ceremony at an Olympic Games, only everyone can win awards at the Judgment Seat of Christ. At that judgment, if you have lived right since you got saved, you will receive rewards. But if you did not live right, then the rewards you could have earned will burn up in front of you. This can either be a wonderful time or an awful time, depending on how you live after you get saved!

8
Now That You Are Saved, What Happens When You Sin?

A lot of new Christians get surprised by something. They ask the Lord into their hearts, and they are as happy as they can be. Then the next day, they do something wrong! Maybe a guy is a roofer. He actually gets saved on Sunday, but then he goes to work on Monday and accidentally smashes his finger with a hammer. Suddenly, he hears a curse word coming out of his mouth, just like he did before he got saved. Oh no! What does that mean? Is he lost again? This is definitely something we need to talk about.

To begin with, let me assure you of something that you might not like to hear: even though you are saved, you are going to sin again at some point. Look at what the Bible says:

Romans 7:18 *For I know that in me (that is, in my flesh,) dwelleth no good thing: for* *to will is present with me; but how to perform that which is good I find not.* **19** *For the good that I would I do not: but the evil which I would not, that I do.* **20** *Now if I do that I would not, it is no more I that do it, but sin that dwelleth in me.* **21** *I find then a law, that, when I would do good, evil is present with me.* **22** *For I delight in the law of God after the inward man:* **23** *But I see another law in my members, warring against the law of my mind, and bringing me into captivity to the law of sin which is in my members.* **24** *O wretched man that I am! who shall deliver me from the body of this death?*

This was written by the apostle Paul, one of the finest Christians that ever lived! Paul had trouble with his "flesh." He was saved, but he found himself still craving sin. You see, as I mentioned earlier, the "inner you," your soul and spirit, is saved and pure. But the "outer you," your body, is still as lost as ever. You do have the Holy Spirit living inside of you, encouraging you to do right and bothering you when you start to do wrong, so you at least stand a fighting chance of living right. But it will be a constant struggle against sinful desires until you get to Heaven!

So, as I said earlier, whether you like it or not, at some point you will sin again. What happens when you do?

The first thing you need to know is that you have not "lost your salvation." You are a child of God. Let me ask you something. Imagine a little girl with a dear mommy. That mommy says, "Do NOT eat any of those cookies in the cookie jar!" For a while, the little girl does right. But after a while, the temptation gets so great, and her mind starts imagining how delicious those cookies would taste. Before you know it, she has gone into the kitchen, plowed into the cookie jar, and devoured the cookies that her mom told her not to eat! Her mom then comes into the kitchen, right as the little girl is eating the very last cookie. The little girl looks up at her mommy in fear, as the mommy looks down at the little girl in anger...

Here is the question: Since the girl disobeyed and took the cookies, has she stopped being her mommy's child? Of course not! She is just as much her mother's daughter as she has always been. Disobeying mommy does not mean that she isn't her daughter anymore!

When you sin and disobey God, it is exactly like that. You became a child of God when you got saved, and that will never change. But something else does change. Let's go back to the story of the cookie thief and find out what it is.

When mommy found daughter in a state of outright disobedience, what do you think happened? Obviously, a good parent is not just going to let that go. Certain things are going to happen. First of all, the daughter will be punished somehow, because willful disobedience always brings punishment from a good parent. This same thing is true of how God will deal with you when you sin after getting saved. The Bible says:

Hebrews 12:6 *For whom the Lord loveth he chasteneth, and scourgeth every son whom he receiveth. 7 If ye endure chastening, God dealeth with you as with sons; for what son is he whom the father chasteneth not?*

That word "chasteneth" means to spank or to discipline. God will punish willful disobedience. When you sin after you get saved, you can expect to be punished. It may be a flat tire or a blown engine or the flu or the loss of something you need or love; it could be anything. But you can be sure that God will let you know *when* it happens, *why* it is happening! People who have been saved for a while have learned that it is not a good idea to disobey, because our Heavenly Father swings a pretty mean switch!

By the way, this is also an excellent test as to whether or not a person truly did get saved. You see, not everyone who comes to an altar to ask God to save them is actually serious about it. Some come because others are doing it, so they don't really get saved. Some come because they don't want to go to Hell, but they also don't want God running their life, and so they don't really get saved either. When a person truly gets saved, he or she has done so not because of what anyone else did, but because they have willingly given control of their life over to God. Paul put it like this:

1 Thessalonians 1:9 *For they themselves shew of us what manner of entering in we had unto you, and* **how ye turned to God from idols to serve the living and true God***;*

That is a very good description of what it means to actually get saved. It is turning from whatever wrong you were doing, turning to God, and giving Him your life so that you can serve Him, meaning that He is your Master!

When a person has truly done this, the things we read above about God spanking them for doing wrong will now happen in his or her life. If a person can continue to sin, enjoy it, and experience no consequences for it, they did not actually get saved! But if you do wrong, then feel miserable about it, and then God spanks you for it until you get right, it is a sure sign that you are actually saved.

Now let's go back to the story of our cookie thief again and learn something else. After the mommy has spanked the daughter for what she did wrong, there are going to be hard feelings between mommy and daughter. Mommy does not like what the daughter did, and the daughter does not like that she got caught and punished. When this happens, even though their relationship as mommy/daughter is still intact, their fellowship is strained. They feel uncomfortable around each other. Something has to happen to fix that. And since the mommy did nothing wrong, the process needs to start with the daughter. Cookie thief needs to go to mommy and apologize. When she does, that good mamma will wrap her arms in love around the daughter, all will be forgiven, and the fellowship will be restored.

It will be exactly like that when you sin now that you have been saved. No other human on Earth may know what you have done, but God will know. And that sweet fellowship you felt with Him right after you got saved will be gone! It will be like He isn't even hearing your prayers, because He isn't! The Bible says:

Psalm 66:18 *If I regard iniquity in my heart, the Lord will not hear me:*

Until you come clean with God, He will ignore your prayers, and you and He will feel very distant from each other.

9

What Kind of Reactions Are You Going to Get?

One thing that often surprises a new Christian is the types of reactions he gets from those that know him. You may be expecting everybody you know to be thrilled to hear that you got saved! But that will probably not be the case. Many will be thrilled, but not everyone.

In Acts 16, a demon possessed girl got saved. You would think that everyone would be thrilled! But the men who had been making money off of this girl were so angry that they tried to kill the ones that led her to the Lord!

When Paul got saved, people were so scared of him that they wouldn't even let him join the church at Jerusalem.

In Muslim countries, when a person gets saved, their family turns them out into the street and has nothing more to do with them.

I am glad that you have gotten saved. But I want you to know that not everyone will be happy about this. For instance, if you hung around with a bunch of sinful buddies, the odds are that they are not going to be too pleased. Once they know that you are not going to drink or party with them, they are likely to get upset!

If you were living with or sleeping with someone you were not married to, when they find out that it is going to stop, they are not likely to be pleased.

But if you really care about those buddies or that person you were living with, then you are going to do right! You see, they are just as lost as you were. If you claim to be saved and then go back and live in sin, you have no chance of winning them to the Lord. You need to do right no matter what the cost and then pray until they get saved too!

Some people will scoff and doubt. Oftentimes it will even be "religious people." They may say, "Well, it won't last. You'll fall back into sin; just wait!" Those kind of people need to be ignored and avoided. If someone is not going to encourage you and help you to live right, stay away from them!

Another thing you will find after you get saved is that, suddenly, people who were never interested in your salvation before are now very interested that you follow them! You will have someone care enough to invite you to a good church, and you will get saved in that good church. Then when you go to work the next morning and tell what happened to you, all of a sudden, the guy at the next machine will say, "Well, I'm a Christian too; come to church with me!" The guy at the next machine never witnessed to you before and never lived like a Christian in front of you, but now, suddenly, he wants you to go to church with him. Stay away from him. If a person didn't care enough to try to win you to the Lord, you don't need to be following them now that you are saved.

Whatever reactions you get, remember that there is only one reaction that matters, and that is how Heaven reacts to you getting saved. Here is how the Bible says that Heaven reacted when you got saved:

Luke 15:10 *Likewise, I say unto you, there is joy in the presence of the angels of God over one sinner that repenteth.*

Heaven rejoiced when you got saved, and we are rejoicing too!

10

Are You Glad You Are Saved? Then Go Win Someone Else!

Have you considered yet the train of events that led to you getting saved? Let me surprise you; that train of events is about 2,000 years long!

Here is what I mean. Somebody won you to the Lord. It may have actually been a few somebodies. It may have been that one person invited you to church, the preacher preached, and somebody else took a Bible at the altar and showed you how to accept Jesus into your heart. Regardless, at least one somebody won you to the Lord!

But that person that won you to the Lord used to be lost, just like you were. How did he or she get saved? Well, somebody won them to the Lord! And before that, somebody won that person to the Lord. And before that...

Do you see what I mean? Somebody got saved back in the days of Jesus. That someone won someone else, who won someone else, who won someone else, who...2000 years later you were won to the Lord! This is exactly how it is supposed to work. The Bible says:

Matthew 28:19 *Go ye therefore, and teach all nations, baptizing them in the name of the Father, and of the Son, and of the Holy Ghost:* **20** *Teaching them to observe all things whatsoever I have commanded you: and, lo, I am with you alway, even unto the end of the world. Amen.*

Mark 16:15 *And he said unto them, Go ye into all the world, and preach the gospel to every creature.*

Proverbs 11:30 *The fruit of the righteous is a tree of life; and* ***he that winneth souls is wise.***

Someone loved you enough to win you to the Lord. Now think about this: is the pastor likely to have a lot of sinful friends? Probably not! He has been saved long enough that most sinners avoid him like the plague! But you? You just got saved. This means that you probably have a better chance of winning people to the Lord than your pastor does!

You may say, "But I have no idea how to do that!" Sure you do. It is a lot less complicated than you think. Just tell everybody what happened to you and then invite them to come to church with you! They will come, the preacher will usually preach about getting saved, and before you know it, you will have been responsible for seeing people you care about get saved. Then they will go get others, and those others will go get others, and you will be responsible for many people not having to go to Hell.

Go get to it!

Made in United States
Orlando, FL
06 October 2024

52422662R00041